I0481515

Litecoin

The Ultimate Litecoin
Cryptocurrency Beginner's Guide.

How To Get Litecoin, Mine It, Keep
It Safe, Trade It And Even Grow It!

RON HELLER

Legal & Disclaimer

The information contained in this book and its contents is not designed to replace or take the place of any form of medical or professional advice; and is not meant to replace the need for independent medical, financial, legal or other professional advice or services, as may be required. The content and information in this book has been provided for educational and entertainment purposes only.

The content and information contained in this book has been compiled from sources deemed reliable, and it is accurate to the best of the Author's knowledge, information and belief. However, the Author cannot guarantee its accuracy and validity and cannot be held liable for any errors and/or omissions. Further, changes are periodically made to this book as and when needed. Where appropriate and/or necessary, you must consult a professional (including but not limited to your doctor, attorney, financial advisor or such other professional advisor)

Table of Contents

Chapter One: What are Cryptocurrencies?

To understand the concept easily, in the contemporary scenario, cryptocurrency, generally, means a digital or virtual currency with the purpose of being used as an alternative medium of payment and receipt for the purchase and selling of products and services. It is relatively a nascent concept of decentralisation, but restricted and applicable provided the exchange system is the same, unlike commodity exchange and stock exchange market. Apparently, various types of cryptocurrencies are being developed to describe the prevailing determining factor of any currency. Almost any kind of cryptocurrency sifts through the process of cryptography in order to regulate, at an informal level, the fabrication and money transfer. Bitcoin was the first ever cryptocurrency formed in 2008 and presented in 2009 (Graydon, 2014).

In 2008, Satoshi Nakamoto was the first person to give birth to this innovative concept. He was the founding member in pioneering the idea of cryptocurrency. Though the mechanics and the framework will be discussed in great length below, just to give a flare and the modus operandi of a cryptocurrency, such as Litecoin; the fiat currency is converted into virtual form and translated into a coin, token or unit, through cryptography. It is significant to mention that the mechanics of safety and privacy are of utmost importance in order to provide accessibility of the keys and digital wallet of Litecoin, provide the rules of cryptography be followed unfailingly (Heller, 2017).

Furthermore, cryptocurrency should only be crafted through the application platform of cryptography for the sole purpose of maintaining security. One of the benefits that Litecoin has that it is near to impossible to forge, unlike circulation of fake currency notes, just because cryptocurrency provides utmost security and features. Secondly, Litecoin has nothing to do with the subtleties of the monetary policy, as it is not issued and nor in control by any federal or central regulator. Lastly, cryptocurrency is immune to any micro and macroeconomic indicators, such as inflation, unemployment, money supply and demand and completely aloof from any governmental tampering. The only thing that it is vulnerable to is that it is vulnerable to any misleading information, speculation and arbitration (Vigna and Casey, 2016).

In order to have the transactions secured through a dedicated cryptocurrency exchange platform, cryptography, this virtual currency or asset is evidently sure to provide safety to the market dealings and inoculate strict control adherences from producing any unnecessary units, and that the transaction has been duly verified from one end to the other. In other words, in the contemporary scenario, during the process of import and export of commodities or services where the exchange of currency takes place (vulnerable to market price fluctuations and cross-currency parity), cryptocurrencies can be used as a substitute or an alternative to the conventional currencies in order to minimise the impact caused due to fluctuation (Surowiecki, 2011).

In the contemporary scenario, where the trend of globalisation and glocatisation is being accepted at an exponential pace by all the developed and developing countries, the notion of cryptocurrency is still hovering in its infancy because, in principle, it is an edict currency. This simply implies that the individuals of the organisation must reach to a mutual agreement in determining the value of any cryptocurrency and under what platform the transactions could take place, such as an established cryptocurrency exchange. For example, if we take Litecoin, the value is established by following the principle of the typical economics of supply and demand rule, implying that it pretty much behaves that of a commodity exchange like coffee beans, crude oil, gold, etc. (Narayanan, et al., 2016).

Crudely putting it, just give the power of determining the value of Litecoin to the people and take the country and its financial regulators out of the scope. Further, he added that each time a Litecoin is transferred or a transaction takes place from one hand to another, it must be duly signed cryptographically by using digital wallets (private keys or codes), whether it be to the public at large or to a specific individual (Oppitz and Tomsu, 2018).

The only negative aspect of doing transactions in cryptocurrencies is that they are nameless, imperceptible and have provided a window of opportunity to smugglers and traffickers. The most primary reason is that it does not fall under the prerogative of any central or federal regulator and they have no power over cryptocurrency users. From this fact it is quite obvious that the individuals or firms who would like to conduct anonymous transactions are very much supportive of the idea of cryptocurrency. Keeping anonymity is the forte of this technology, but in essence, the sole purpose is to transfer the power of determining the value of goods from organisation to people, despite the fact that it can be abused for illegal purposes as well (Litke and Stewart, 2014).

The history of cryptocurrency goes back to as far as 1998, when Wei Dai published an article, narrating the fervours of a confidential electronic transaction system by the name of B-Money (Sharma, Krishma, and Raina, 2017).

Litecoin entered the colosseum of cryptocurrency in 2011 through the platform GitHub, the brainchild of Charlie Lee (an ex-employee of Google). GitHub is primarily a computer code generator and also follows the functionality of Source Code Management (SCM). In terms of cryptographic hash function, it was the first one to successfully deploy a scrypt instead of SHA-256 (Chen et al., 2017).

By the end of 2013, the total price value of a Litecoin underwent an exponential increase in the price touching the stratosphere by two-fold in a day and aggregate market capitalisation reached One Billion USD. Gradually it the market capitalisation soared to, approximately, USD 4.6 billion or in other words USD85 per token. In May 2017, with the quick turnaround time of completing the transaction of Litecoin (as opposed to that of Bitcoin), the market capitalisation of the coin rocketed to USD 18 billion.

Though Litecoin and Bitcoin have been designed using the cryptography they do differ, essentially, in two ways.

Firstly with regards to transactions or blocks, the exchange is completed in short span of 2 and ½ minutes as opposed to the transaction in the framework of Bitcoin, which takes about 10 minutes. Hence the authentication of a transaction on the Litecoin network is much quicker and the onus goes to implementing the process of SegWit.

Secondly and as earlier mentioned, while designing Litecoin, its founder used scrypt as an algorithmic function in the development of Proof of Work (discussed in detail in the book), which in essence is a sequential memory-hard function and consuming more memory as opposed to developing a hash algorithm. This makes mining an expensive and sophisticated proposition in the case of Litecoin as opposed to Bitcoin, which uses hash algorithmic functionality through the platform of SHA-256.

2.0 Chapter Two: Why Litecoin?

With the international scenario inoculating the notion of globalisation, swift adaptation towards a digital-based economic system is inevitable. Previously Credit Cards replaced fiat currency in the form of paperless money. Bank statements, news article, shopping and transactions are transcending to a paperless form. The concept of digital banking, digital marketing, buying and selling, online shopping and e-books is not only being environmentally friendly but also swift and only a touch away. The most recent story is the advent of cryptocurrency. The most talked about an innovative additive to the digital and virtual payment industry (Xiang, et al., 2017).

Crypto is developed for the sole purpose of trading digital information; just like any other fiat currency and this is where the main difference lies. Cryptocurrency can be considered as an alternative to fiat currency, which exploits the science of cryptography to ensure that its blockchain technology is secure and making it near to impossible to counterfeit. Since it does not fall within the purview of some central regulatory framework, hence no country or law can deprive you of it.

In the past couple of years, Bitcoin and Litecoin have been in the spotlight of public and general market enthusiasts and there are good reasons behind it. Some of the important features are:

- Firstly, committing fraud is improbable, unless you abuse the concept of crypto cloud mining. All features of Bitcoin and Litecoin are heavily ciphered and at the same time complex and sophisticated. The sole purpose of going through this process of securing the identity and transaction is to assure the genuineness of recordkeeping.

- Since Blockchain uses a Secure Hash Algorithm (SHA-256 algorithm) and Litecoin uses a scrypt, the identity of buyers, sellers and transaction are anonymous; hence, there is no chance theft of pilferage of personal data. The data-mart assures that all the exchanges and transaction will be operated by a key or through digital wallets. At the backend, all the transactions are examined to ensure that the current user authentically owns anyone who uses the coins. The so-called technological process is also known as blockchain (Kowkutla and Ravi, 2017).

- In the above section, we mentioned the concept of digital wallets. These wallets can be called either Hot Wallets or Cold Wallets. Both are digital in nature, however, the primary difference is that a hot wallet is connected to the crypto exchange through an internet and cold wallet (also known as a hardware wallet is not.

- If one has most of your coins is in the hot wallet, then it is vulnerable to hacks and cyber-attacks since you need to be connected to the internet at all times.

- On the other hand, the hot wallet is comparatively safer because it is offline and stored in a hardware peripheral. However, on a need basis, you can plug in the hot wallet to the computer as required. Secondly, the transactions are more secure because the one needs to press the tab on the hardware device while confirming the transaction on the crypto exchange.

- One of the hot wallets is Trezor with superior customer experience. Asides that it also supports various cryptos, such as Bitcoin and Litecoin.

- Since you are the owner of the cryptocurrency, therefore it is decentralised. No regulator, law or legislative government, even bank, has any dominance over it.

- Blockchain Management offers a persistent affirmation that all digital transactions are secure and encrypted. Smart contracts or e-contracts, transactions between two users, make the identity of the users and entities completely anonymous; therefore, the entire platform cannot be hacked and is void of any cyber-attacks or digital fraud (Verma, et al, 2017).

With three billion people on the planet having access to the internet, cryptocurrency exchange is a safe haven for them, as it does not demand adherence to the conventional stock and commodity exchange. Such individuals and firms are starting to enter the cryptocurrency market. It is valued that the blockchain economy is above one hundred billion dollars and vastly untapped (Hegadekatti and SG, 2017).

With umpteen numbers of cryptos entering the market, reliance on one coin is an invitation to bring an investor on the road. Hence, it is imperative to have diversification in one's investment portfolio in relation to crypto.

Having a diversified portfolio is one of the fundamental principles that any investor has to adhere, prudently. Some coins are good for short-term investment, while others are best if remained for safekeeping on a long-term basis. In doing so, one not only diversifies the portfolio but also spreads the risks associated with it, just in case if one of the investment crashes.

When you invest in numerous types of investment instruments, with various levels of associated risk: an individual a decreases the probability for any of the assets to crash in proportion to the overall price value of the portfolio. It helps the individual to increase the option of vesting in an asset, whose yield or return is better and acclimatise the portfolio mix in accordance with the risk and profit.

In the recent past, conventional portfolio mix comprised of shares, bonds, and property, but with the advent of crypto, more money makers are innovating new portfolio mix. In order to add diversification to the portfolio mix by including crypto can have its pros and cons. A few of them are mentioned below:

Advantages

Security. Although most of the investors are sceptical in being exposed to virtual currency, online transaction (using the blockchain technology as they are secure). Being nascent in nature it is might still be vulnerable to gaps, but with blockchain technology embedded in its DNA, crypto is one hundred percent hack-proof, irreversible and invulnerable to cyber-attacks.

Potential. The foremost purpose of crypto is decentralisation and deregulation, where corporate governance is not under any central jurisdiction or reserve banks. The underlying potential is huge, where you have to document the in-flows and out-flows of them as an integral part of the cash/money system in order to comply with the AML and KYC requirements. In the case of cryptocurrency there is no such need, thus an exponential benefit is waiting for the investor to unearth.

Independence. Because it is decentralised and not tied to any one government, physical asset, market or central regulators, the people have foremost authority to determine the price value of the coin.

To fortify the statement made above, Litecoin and other cryptocurrencies are absolutely liberated from other systems, such as government intermediation, monetary policy and regulators' compliance. Which implies, theoretically, cryptocurrency is of more value as a diversified investment and does not have any relationship (linear or non-linear) to any of the conventional assets.

Disadvantages

Current trend. Despite being prone to reward halving and volatile, Bitcoin's price value, as opposed to Litecoin, is at its acme. According to some financial experts the price of Bitcoin may have no bounds on the value of Bitcoin has appreciated faster as opposed to the actual value, but some believe that this phase is at the initial junction of a financial bubble and eventually, in the future not so soon could plunge the plummet the value to rock-bottom. In simple words, investors who have a high or complete investment in Bitcoin may turn out to be a risky proposition. Hence, it is wise; to diversify your crypto portfolio, by vesting an equivalent part into Litecoin (which has shown a stable trend in the last one year).

Volatility. Even if the price is not a financial bubble, you should know that the newness and excitement around cryptocurrencies make them a highly volatile investment. It is almost certain that the price will fluctuate up and down, sometimes wildly, before it stabilises. For low-risk investors, this should be a red flag.

Uncertainty. Cryptocurrencies are still in its infancy and legislature is not at ease on how to tackle or regulate them. In many countries, their respective stock exchange commissions (SEC) have initiated to forbid Initial Coin Offerings (discussed in detail below) and trading of virtual currencies. It is too premature and uncertain to provide any substantial conjecture about their scope in future.

3.0 Chapter Three: Historical Trend and Future Outlook

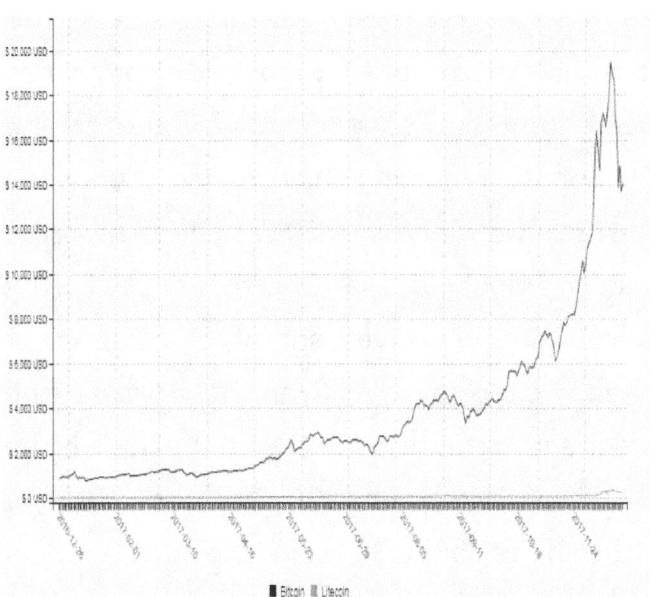

$20,000 USD

$18,000 USD

$16,000 USD

$14,000 USD

$12,000 USD

$10,000 USD

$8,000 USD

$6,000 USD

$4,000 USD

$2,000 USD

$0 USD

■ Bitcoin ■ Litecoin

What was discussed in the above chapter can be substantiated by the fact, if we look at the historical trend of Litecoin and Bitcoin? If we look at the trend of the price value of coins of both Bitcoin and Litecoin, the pattern emerges out to be:

In the above table, we see the price volatility of Bitcoin and Litecoin. In Dec 2016, the price value of Bitcoin was USD 905.14 and of Litecoin, it was USD 4.42. In a one-year span, the price value of Bitcoin jumped to USD 14,029.86 (with an all-time high at USD 19,453.35). However, if you look a closer look at the trend of Bitcoin, the price has been through frequent troughs and crests. Exponential volatility (upward trend between the last two months of 2017) and then in the last fortnight of the December 2017, the price value nosedived sharply. On the other hand, Litecoin displayed a stable and stagnant trend. However, in the last three weeks of December 2017, the price value of Litecoin exhibited a modest and a gradual growth.

Bitcoin is a nail-biter; keep the investor on the ledge. In financial terms, can the growth and price value of Bitcoin be deemed as a financial bubble? However, it is too premature to give a verdict on the price aspect of Bitcoin. Whereas investors of Litecoin do have a sense of peace and know that, it is not susceptible to any price volatility. It is important here to mention that Litecoin is the second best-traded crypto, just because that it is not only a risky asset and the also provides quick turnaround time for authentication of transactions.

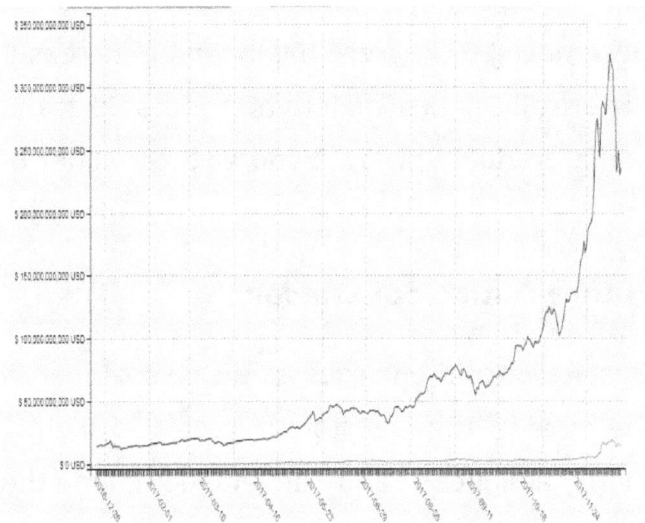

In the below table, we will compare the market capitalisation of both Bitcoin and Litecoin. Last year, Bitcoin's market capitalisation was USD 14.540 billion

and of Litecoin it was merely USD 216 million. In the last week of Dec 2017, the market capitalisation of Bitcoin soared to USD 235.17 billion (with an all-time high at USD 325.792 billion) and Litecoin's market capitalisation increased to USD 15.095 billion. One thing that can be deduced is that the expansion of Litecoin is not a financial bubble. Looking closely at Litecoin's market capitalisation in the last few weeks of December 2017, there has been an increase. Historically it has maintained a stable trend and a gradual upward trend at the twilight of 2017.

Future Outlook of Litecoin

Despite Bitcoin emerges as a sky-scrapper in the eyes of the investors, Litecoin is slightly more advanced and developed than the former. For instance and as earlier mentioned, the turnaround time for authenticating/completing the transaction in Litecoin is faster than Bitcoin. The validation time of a transaction in Litecoin is two and a half minutes as compared to Bitcoin's ten minutes. This is because Litecoin uses the platform of Lightning Network in order to develop a block by filtering it through SegWit (discussed in detail in the following chapter). It is due to SegWit (Segregated Witness) that the process of completing the transaction in Litecoin is swift as compared to Bitcoin and the reason is that Bitcoin has not embedded the process of SegWit into its technology.

The only drawback is that when it comes to crypto mining, Litecoin rewards 25 coins for each block, whereas Bitcoin pays half of that. This could be a drawback, but when it comes to crypto mining, the miners are enthusiastic about Litecoin.

Although these petty issues may seem meagre, initially, they can have a substantial impact on price value forecast of Litecoin.

The price value of Litecoin is dependent on two aspects, which are popularity and accessibility. In order to so, Litecoin must capture a respective share of investors (entities and individual) to rationalise its existence on a long-term basis. At the same time, provide ease of accessing the units in order to conduct the transaction. One of the aspects successfully fulfilled the requirements in the early part of 2017 in addition to Bitcoin and Ethereum.

4.0 Chapter Four: Scope of Litecoin

Ever since Litecoin implemented SegWit into its process of trading, it has gained vivid prominence among crypto investors and traders. However, it is essential that before diving into the crypto exchange pool of trading, it is wise that the investor becomes familiar with few of the below-mentioned connotations:

Blockchain Management or Blockchain Technology

Blockchain Management is the foremost skeleton in the development of Litecoin or any other crypto. Blockchain Management is a merger of two words, i.e. block and chain. In the cosmos of digital currency, a "block" implies as a "transaction or set of transactions" and "chain" is the nexus through which each block is linked. When we talk about technology or management, it denotes that the transaction or group of transactions are chained together in a chronological order. Only authenticated transactions or "blocks" can become a part of the blockchain. This ensures that the trade is not fake nor it is erroneously duplicated. The validation process relies on the data which is encrypted by employing an algorithm, which complex and sophisticated, both mathematically and statistically. (O'Leary, et al, 2017).

Two primary factors give Litecoin leverage over the traditional blockchain management. Firstly it does not deploy a hash algorithm, rather it uses the scrypt algorithm. In addition, both these algorithms are used to validate transactions. However, there are certain differences between them

As earlier stated, a hash algorithmic function is more sophisticated and used by Bitcoin. Since it uses hash functionality, the processing of the block is slow. An average turnaround time for a block to get authenticated is about 10 minutes in the case of Bitcoin. When it comes to crypto mining of coins by using the hash algorithm, hash rates frequently necessitates hash difficulty at gigahashes per second (GH/s) scale or greater. At times the hash difficulty is computed in terrahashes per second (TH/s) or one trillion hash computations per second and petahashes per second (PH/s), or one quadrillion hash computations per second. Or to put it simply, the higher the hash difficulty, more the energy (electricity) is consumed with the costly high-end configuration of computer components and related paraphernalia.

Scrypt is relatively quicker and was made an integral part while designing Litecoin. Scrypt is simpler to process on an existing personal desktop and is cost-effective as it consumes less power and energy as opposed to SHA-256. Litecoin mining is much preferable option for most of the miners. Litecoin mining is also successful because the scrypt hash rates fall in the domain of kilohashes per second (KH/s) or megahashes per second (MH/s). The hash difficulty can easily be deduced with normal desktops or laptops, without incurring any high-cost expenditure while procuring computer-related peripherals.

Sidechains and SegWit

In a nutshell, sidechain is an impartial ledger, cryptographic in nature, and is connected to the primary blockchain without disturbing the performance and rate. They are designed just to augment the absorption capacity of the prevalent blockchain technology. It has been witnessed by many miners that already established blockchains are expanding with regards to alphanumeric digits and storage capacity. Hence increasing the hash difficulty for the miners and the owners to sustain the colossal cobweb of cryptocurrency. In order to overcome this issue of blockchain limitation, sidechain offers a much easy solution. Sidechain has the ability to increase the capacity of the system by creating an interoperable blockchain skeleton. In layman terms, sidechain is essentially a parallel chain that tracks along with the primary blockchain.

Litecoin was the first crypto to embed SegWit (Segregated Witness) by using the platform of "Lightning Network" in its core design. With this, Litecoin is able to amplify the limit size of the block in a blockchain by separating (Segregating) the digital signature from the transaction data. On the backend, this process allows freeing space to adjoin more transactions (block) to the existing blockchain.

SegWit is not part of the Bitcoin technology and eventually, it will become very difficult for Bitcoin users to conduct the transaction. As earlier stated that it takes 10 minutes to validate a transaction or block before it could be added to the existing blockchain. Bitcoin, being one of the most traded cryptocurrencies in the market, just imagine that a new block is being added to the blockchain after every ten minutes. Since the capsize of one block is restricted to 1MB, only required transactions become part of the blockchain. Slowly and gradually the space limit and size of the blockchain eat up many parts of the bandwidth and network, resulting in turndown time while processing and validating the transactions. Although Bitcoin stands by its affirmation that the validation process takes 10 minutes but in some instances, it can devour hours before authenticating a valid transaction.

Based on the above postulation, it can be deduced that if Bitcoin wants to survive on a long-term basis, its network needs to go through a drastic change.

This is the benefit that Litecoin has in its technology but a big drawback for Bitcoin.

Proof of Work

Proof of Work (PoW) in reality is a levelled field to inspire and influence miners to come up with a precise hash. The likelihood of reaching a plausible solution is not very high. Hence whenever a miner validates a block, he is subsequently. The award depends on the crypto itself. In case of Litecoin, the miner is incentivised by 25 units, whereas Bitcoin pays 12.5 units. On a broader aspect, they can also be awarded through fiat currency also (Bissias and Levine, 2017).

PoW is a modus operandi whose objective is to dissuade hacking and spamming in the form of Distributed Denial of Service Attack (DDoS). During the process of mining or creating a block, it has the ability to drain all the sources of a personal computer by bombarding several shams requestions.

The notion of PoW was already in existence, afore to the inception of Bitcoin but nevertheless, it became part of Bitcoin's technology. As a matter of fact, the framework of PoW was conceptualised by Cynthia Dwork and Moni Naor in 1993. However, the terminology of proof of work was claimed by Markus Jakobsson and Ari Juels in 1999. Coming back to 2017, PoW is still remembered as an essential feature of Bitcoin as it permits distrusted and uncirculated unanimity. In simple words, a trustless and distributed consensus implies that in any transaction, an individual does not have to be dependent on third-parties. In cryptocurrencies, whenever a transaction takes place, the relevant parties will also get an e-copy of the blockchain and the person can verify the transaction independently.

Proof of Stake

As opposed to PoW, PoS is an alternative type of algorithmic hash to secure the blockchain. PoS is one of the other ways of resolving the issue of security for miners with respect to the number of coins at disposal (Vranken, 2017).

So to encapsulate in all, PoS is another way of authenticating the transactions and also allows a trustless and distributed consensus, just like in the case of PoW. The goal of PoW and PoS is the same, but the methodology in approaching the end objective differs.

Unlike PoW, there is no block reward in PoS. Instead, the miner is rewarded by charging fees per transaction. The reason for this difference is that in PoW have to mine the block by solving complex mathematical equations with the objective of authenticating transactions and generating new blocks. PoS, on the other hand, chooses the miner of the new block in a definitive way, relevant to the stake or wealth of the block.

5.0 Chapter Five: Litecoin Mining

Crypto Mining is an integral part of the cryptocurrency industry, but it is vital to discover other alternate ways to authenticate the transactions taking place. This can be done by diving into a series of complicated mathematical and statistical equations in order to complete the entire data structure of a blockchain (Hsieh, Vergne and Wang, 2017).

Eventually, this made to one gigantic setback. It initially started out with the scarcity of human resource who had the expertise of solving such types of equations. If this problem were remedied instantly, the entire structure of blockchain would come tumbling down. Therefore, to offer benefits to such people in solving the equations, they are now reimbursed into the same cryptocurrency that they are validating. Finally, making crypto mining a profitable ventures (Peterson, 2017).

After the person gets a good grip on crypto mining, it is probable that you start your business of crypto mining and be your own owner. You earn handsomely, do not need to declare anything to the tax authorities and enjoy the freedom as long as it lasts.

The main quarrel regarding cryptocurrency is with the country's financial regulatory framework. But eventually, the transactions conducted under the ambit of cryptocurrency continues to remain anonymous and untraceable, therefore providing the privacy to the identity of a crypto miner on how much money are they minting and for what purpose they using (Sheehan, et al, 2017).

To sum it all up crypto mining can be a tremendous incentive feature, with all of the benefits above.

Cryptocurrency, such as Litecoin make their way into the market through the process call Crypto Mining. In this overall activity, it is imperative that engagement of a user with computer and internet is in place at all times. Secondly, their details can be verified by assigning unique keys or digital wallets and allows the payments to be stored into a data warehouse for mining. (Solat and Potop-Butucaru, 2017).

While a mining a block in the case of Litecoin, the miner has to comply with certain guidelines. They usually comprise of an array of steps in sequential and chronological order to motivate the miner to be a part of a competitive environment. Furthermore, the miner is given with unlimited and unimaginable CPU configuration to deduce a hash that is aligned to the requirements using any of the available algorithmic function.

In deriving a scrypt, one has to follow a predetermined process which essentially is a one-way street. Once you enter the domain of deducing the hash, there is no going back. Almost all the miners are in the probe for a plausible solution the matches the criteria, no matter how many and how much equipments are required. Plus they need to make it difficult and impossible to decipher, which in other words is also called proof of work (DiPiero, 2017).

Crypto Cloud Mining is somewhat similar to that of crypto mining with one basic difference, which is provided in detail ahead. It would relatively be an easy ask if considering the example of Bitcoin's mining process, which uses a data centre, in a remote location and pooling in the electricity consumed by the processors at associated peripherals. In other words, instead of mining by a particular individual, the process is outsourced or contracted to a third-party, typically an organisation who can bear the burden of the cost of electricity and central processing units (CPU), who does all the mining of Litecoin on behalf of the users without using their own computers (Qui, et al., 2017).

Designing a scyrpt algorthimic function is much need of the day for Litecoin as it empowers the miners to provide secured encrytion in crafting a new block. Subsequently, hashing demands exponential

CPU output on a mass scale, thus leading to increase in expenses. It is vital to mention here that miners are awarded only if the created hash matches the requirements and criteria, specified in terms and conditions. (Mitzenmacher, 2017).

With any other nascent innovative products and solutions, there are inherent benefits and inherent risks related to cloud mining, which the user need to bear in mind before investing (Shmueli, et al., 2017):

Advantages of Cloud Mining

- With no chilling towers and cooling fans, the home becomes a haven of calmness and tranquillity. As the miners, while using an algorithmic hash, the CPU tends to be in constant use and the motherboard becomes hot and in order to prevent any hardware meltdown, it needs to operate in a cold environment. With Litecoin, unless one wants to venture into pool mining, one can easily process the mining on a home-based CPU.

- To prevent the constant running of cooling equipment, the cost of electricity has high tendency to increase. Nearly all users cannot afford to bear the high cost, which is why organisation involved in crypto mining comes into play.

- As soon as miners discover that that cloud mining is a profitable venture, then disposing of any hardware becomes next to impossible.

- Since firms involved in cloud mining can afford to purchase chilling towers and equipment, problems related to aeration are ruled out.

Disadvantages of Cloud Mining

1. Some cloud mining functions tend to commit fraud when the miners or users also share information regarding their keys and digital wallet.

2. In cloud mining, the operations of miners become vulnerable and transparent.

3. There is no control and suppleness in cloud mining.

You need to know about a few technical stuff about creating a mining rig before you actually start mining. Using a CPU for mining is slowly and gradually becoming obsolete and being replaced by Graphics Processing Unit (GPU). The new technology provides a quicker path for deciphering the alogorithms to produce more coins. When it comes to crypto mining or crypto cloud mining, GPUs must be the main focal point in developing a mining rig. During the process of mining, configuration for mining Bitcoin will be the same for any crypto who runs on SHA-256 algorithm functionality. The same goes for Litecoin and all those cryptos using scrypt algorithm functionality. Preferably, the ATI HD 7950 card's graphics card is the most preferable option for miners, as it provides the most reasonable value-for-value, if you are mining on a shoe-string budget. Gradually, there is always a probability of upgrading your hardware peripherals. Essentially there are three thing that one should worry about when you constructing a mining rig:

- Graphics Card: Never ever compromise on purchasing a cheap graphics card. Go for the most high geared one.

- Power Supply: Consumption of electricity is extremely high. Requirement of adequate uninterrupted power supply is must. For exampe, for mining a rig, requirement of two or three graphics cards, it is essential one does not compromise anything 1000w plus.

- Motherboard: The minimum requirements are atleast three slots in the motherboard.

- Upgraded and Licenses Operating System.

- In mining, one does not require a RAM more than 8GB, otherwise, carbon will start to residue on the slots.

- Since all the activities will be performed through the internet, substantial space on hard drive is not important.

- If a mining rig is not encased in a unit it is better. As the process of mining generally heats up the rig and in that case one must think of installing chilling and cooling towers to lower down the temperature to avoid any crash.

Cloud mining is primarily a service provider and if they are mining the blockchain, obviously they are going to charge something in return, which implies that it can less profitable for the miner or the user.

Ideally, cloud mining is meant for those people who do not have the time, are not tech-savvy and neither they own any cryptocurrency-related equipment. In addition, if you are based in a country where the electricity costs are scoring high, then its prudent to subcontract your mining operation to an organisation, which is located in a country where the costs are comparatively lower.

There is another offshoot in the field of mining, commonly known as Multi-pool Mining. It is the concept of hopping or trading from one type of cryptocurrency to another cryptocurrency and then taking into consideration that which coin trade mining is profitable in that course of the period.

Miners who indulge in multi-pooling will first and most will consider that cryptocurrency network, which has the lowest mining power in terms of cost and their exchange rates is lucrative. Ideally and to put it prudently the miner will sell their minted crypto or any other fiat currency into the token issued by Bitcoin, only to depreciate the value of crypto which they have just mined (Sun, Qin and Ma, 2017).

To illustrate it in a better way, for example, what a miner will do in multi- pooling is that the miner will consider that specific cryptocurrency, based upon the total mining power. For instance currently, a crypto has a combined mining consumption of 100 GH. The miner will then compute the power required to run a hash algorithmic function, which in this case the assumption is 900GH. What it basically implies is that the miners have a ninety percent probability of mining a block (set of the transaction) provided the miners are willing to hop onto the hash rate or hash power to 900GH or even into peta hashes. However, unlike Bitcoin, Litecoin is much easier to mine as it does not require expensive components (large scale capital expenditure) and can be done on personal computers.

6.0 Chapter Six: Trading and Exchange of Litecoin

Prior we try to explore the process of crypto trading, it is important that one must have a digital wallet and an online exchange platform, where the trading of one cryptocurrency can be traded with another one. Let us first understand in detail the concept of a cryptocurrency exchange in detail. Speaking, broadly, there are four types of crypto trading platforms (Mokhtarian and Lindgren, 2017):

Conventional Cryptocurrency Exchange

In such types of online platforms, they follow the mechanism of the prevalent stock and commodity exchange. A platform where trading is conducted among the buyers, sellers and an intermediary source on the basis of the current market price of any cryptocurrency. For each transaction, the middleman charges a certain percentage of commission. The fee can either be in the shape of an acceptable currency or a cryptocurrency. Online platforms, such as

Coinbase's GDAX, Bittrex, Binance, Kraken and Shapeshift are few of those. For example, if one wants to convert or encash a cryptocurrency into any foreign currency, they can easily utilise the facilities being offered by such exchange (Bianchi, 2017).

Direct Trading Exchange

Such online exchanges trade directly and there is no concept of an intermediary. The buyers and sellers trading without any intermediary and secondly the seller determine their own cross-currency parity and do not use some absolute market price.

Cryptocurrency Brokers

To facilitate the go buyers and seller, there are web-based portals and applications for cryptocurrency exchange. They allow the convenience of having access to trade via either smartphone, tablets or a desktop. These websites play the role of a stockbroker, where the prices are already fixed to purchase and offloading cryptocurrencies (Corbet, et al., 2017).

Cryptocurrency Funds

One way of trading cryptocurrencies is through a pool of funds, which are managed by professionals, in order to facilitate the masses to purchase and sell cryptocurrency through the means of a fund. These are meant for investors who want to purchase the cryptocurrencies and hold them for a long period, like GBTC (Zima, 2017).

It is imperative to mention that an online platform for crypto exchange is not a part a conventional stock exchange. Although the mechanics are most or less the same but the main difference lies in their nature of trade and portals.

It is proposed that for an amateur or a fresh entrant, should initiate cryptocurrency trade either through a fund like GBTC. It is a cryptocurrency fund that possesses its mostly trades in Litecoin and Bitcoin, in a way it acts as an intermediary in a professional way instead of some amateur getting involved into crypto trade directly and become vulnerable to losses (Krause and Pham, 2017).

On the other hand, the Coinbase is another crypto trading platform and is user-friendly. The only limitation is that it only trades in Bitcoin, Ethereum, and Litecoin. Speaking of facts the trade of Litecoin was frantically erratic in the past five year. At a point in time, either you become filthy rich or incur a massive loss, whether it be in any cryptocurrency. It is suggested that while trading in cryptocurrencies, one must not concentrate on just one, but a mixture of Bitcoin, Ethereum and Litecoin. On the other hand, the second option is to go employ the service of GBTC to mitigate any risks and take precautionary measures (Krause and Pham, 2017).

When discussing cryptocurrency, it is irrefutable not to mention Litecoin. It has emerged as one of the instrumental crypto in the crypto exchange and trading market that can pose a serious threat to Bitcoin trading because of its swift transaction dealing. It has become a formidable choice when it comes to having a diversified portfolio of cryptocurrencies. In the past few years, Litecoin was considered an underestimated crypto on the trading platform, despite having a unique plus point over Bitcoin and a prominent contender to the latter.

Ever since 2017, Litecoin adopted the protocol process of SegWit, it has become more efficient than Bitcoin. However, there are gossips among the crypto traders that Bitcoin was in the process of implementing SegWit2x but due to insufficient consensus by the mining sector, it was put on the backburner. To further augment It there are no news as to when Bitcoin adopts the upgrades. The cryptocurrency underwent market correction and substantial fluctuation crested against the trading and exchange reef of Bitcoin. Whereas, the price value of Litecoin also felt the tremor in the same period but it was marginal, but Bitcoin is still sensing the aftershocks.

The ideal approach to purchase Litecoin is via a cryptocurrency exchange, which are in hundred, but Coinbase (if it is present in your nation) is the most preferred one. Due to liquidity issues, it is not easy to purchase coins using a fiat currency, but Litecoin being one of pioneers in cryptocurrencies it has ample liquidity and it is virtually probable to buy the coin in exchange with USD, EURO, CNY, etc.

The only apprehension is exchanges, via intermediary, can be a risky proposition. To safeguard your assets and investments is your responsibility, whether the market witness a bearish or bullish trend.

In essence, there are two road to purchase or trade Litecoin. If the priority is to trade the fiat currency for Litecoin, then Coinbase is the preferred option among all other exchanges. Coinbase deals in various fiat currencies and you can use credit cards too to purchase the coins. The only cost is the variable surcharge fee, depending on credit cards or internal transfer of bank funds.

Coinbase needs ID verification and correspondence address during registration as a generic process. This helps in prevent the exchange platform from illegal laundering of money and related transactions. Those users, who want to seal their identity and benefit from the feature of anonymity, will resort to take an alternate path.

The alternate route is to buy Bitcoin first via peer-to-peer exchange, as it does not need ID for verification. In this type of exchange, LocalBitcoins is preferable, which permits the users to purchase Bitcoin with almost any mode of currency. When you wallet the Bitcoins they can be traded for Litecoins at different exchange but it is vital to ensure that the user are rigorously vetted. It has been observed that certain dodgy users manipulate this platform to swindle new users, who have just entered the crypto exchange market. For new Litecoin users it is important to enable the two-factor process of authorisation and avoid keeping all your coins in the hot wallet. Do not share access codes of both the wallets (hot and cold) and password under any circumstances. Since you need to have an internet-connected peripheral (CPU or Mobile Phone), ensure that all the passwords are adequately secured.

During trading and exchange incidents, like phishing scams and cyber-attacks, hackers found loopholes in the exchanges and wallets of Bitcoin. Millions of dollars were swindled and exchanges went bankrupt. Fortunately, there is always Litecoin to the rescue, which has taken measures to prevent such instances and keep on briefing the users regarding preventive measures.

7.0 Chapter Seven Litecoin Arbitrage:

In the term of lexigraphy, arbitrage is essentially a riskless transaction when you purchase something, when the price or value is low, and sell when the price has skyrocketed in a quick span of time. In the contemporary scenario, in stock exchanges, such a transaction is typically referred as short selling and it is a practice, which many investors and brokers discourage.

Markets or exchanges, which are dominated by opinion leaders at times, conduct transactions that arbitrage or speculative in nature, whether it is a stock exchange, commodity exchange or cryptocurrency exchange (Cheun, et al., 2017).

In order to have a vivid sense let us assume that we take two countries, such as ABC and XYZ. The government of ABC announces a news, publicly mentioning that they have put a ban on the Litecoin Trading for life. This will trigger panic amongst the buyer and they will gradually offload all the coins and convert them to a fiat currency. Such a gossip and leads to complete offloading of the tokens and consequently the entire market cryptocurrency crashes. However, owners of cryptocurrency in XYZ, where people are still sleeping and completely unaware of the panicking situation in the crypto exchange of ABC country are not able to take preventive measures against this stir. It is imperative to mention that the market has still not opened in XYZ country and the price value of cryptocurrency remains unstirred.

What it implies. If an individual is a sharp-minded person with quick decision making abilities and knows how the crypto exchange markets function, the person will purchase the cryptocurrency at the plummeted value in ABC country and without wasting any time. The same person at the same time will sell all the coins in the crypto exchange in the XYZ country. The particular individual has not only earned a handsome profit but also indulged in the act of arbitration.

Therefore, in essence, the platform of crypto trading and crypto exchange provide a huge window of opportunity in the shape of crypto arbitrage. Below are some of the opportunities along with examples (Walker, 2017).

1.   The cryptocurrency market is in its infancy. In 2010, the first official Bitcoin exchange opened its doors, as opposed to the conventional stock market, which was commenced its operations in 1642. In the conventional stock exchange, the transfer of information is slow and there are few buyers and sellers, therefore the level of competition is low. In a cryptocurrency trading and exchange, you are the first person when it comes to arbitration due to fast-paced communication.

2.   You cannot rule out the possibility of volatility in a cryptocurrency market. In

reality, a normal person would consider it a bad proposition. On the other hand, a user who utilises this volatility as an opportunity to conduct an arbitrage exchange will be excited. In totality, the arbitrage trading, a traditionally risky investment turns cryptocurrency exchange into a riskless endeavour and ensures that there is consistency in profitability.

Types of Arbitrage

Apparently, this is not easy as it sounds. Users have deduced complex mix of strategies to overpower others. A few of these can be labelled as (Yu and Zhang, 2017):

1.   *Simple arbitrage* is trading in the same coin at the same time.

2.   *Triangular arbitrage* is simply seizing the opportunity of difference in cross-currency parity. Such as the example cited above ABC and XYZ country.

3.   *Convergence   arbitrage* is   where things get interesting. It takes about short selling in true essence. You offload the Litecoins at a high value, wait until the price of Litecoins comes down and at the same time, you buy back all the coins at a lower price (perhaps additional tokens), hence the profit that you have earned is almost equivalent to the amount during convergence.

4.   *Future Index Arbitrage:* A few crypto exchanges, for example, Bitmex, offer you the liberty to purchase Litecoin on a futures contract. This is slightly a more complex crypto arbitrage in nature. Since the coins are being traded on futures, buying or selling, you will need to quote the pricing of the coin by a factor in the rate of interest in accordance with the period.

Crypto Arbitrage provides you with the opportunity to make profits instantaneously, provided you have first-hand information. Always keep in mind that crypto markets are still nascent and there are ample of opportunities available.

Conclusion

In the end, the outlook of cryptocurrency will be dividing the Litecoin block by two. This will be, perhaps, the foremost happening and an erratic era in the overall history of Litecoin. The concept of block (set of transactions) reward halving was built into the genetic structure of Litecoin by its developer; following the legacy of Bitcoin. In essence, its purpose is to make Litecoin vulnerable to devaluation. Primarily it implies that the quantity of tokens of Litecoin, currently in circulation, will be reduced. This is something inevitable to the fate of Litecoin. Therefore, in essence, it can be predicted with the passage of time, the value of Litecoin will increase and coin in circulation will decrease.

However, it is also imperative to mention here that unlike conventional trading of shares in a stock exchange, it will be challenging task for the users of cryptocurrencies. The prime reason is that they not only need to have the awareness and knowledge related to technology, but also need to understand the mechanics of mining, exploiting opportunity in crisis (in the event of arbitrage) and be very cautious in trading crypto in futures market. Conducting exchange through hedging or in futures, can be a financial bubble in disguise and in the situation of cryptocurrencies, such as Litecoin, can drive the investor from the roof to the streets in a matter of hours. Therefore, it is suggested that the portfolio mix should not be concentrated on one particular type of coin or token. Predominantly, the value of crypto behaves well as per the essence of a capital market as opposed to commodity or money market. In other words, the future trend can lead to panic but it does not mean that an individual goes berserk, just stay calm, provided you have tailored your mind-set as per the knowledge and become well-versed in all kind of connotations.

References

Atzori, M., (2016). *Blockchain-based architectures for the internet of things*: A survey.

Bianchi, D., (2017). *Cryptocurrencies as an Asset Class*: An Empirical Assessment.

Bissias, G. and Levine, B.N., (2017). Bobtail: *A Proof-of-Work Target that Minimizes Blockchain Mining Variance* (Draft). arXiv preprint arXiv:1709.08750.

Bradbury, D., (2015). In blocks [security bitcoin]. *Engineering & Technology, 10*(2), pp.68-71.

Chen, S., Chen, C.Y.H., Härdle, W.K., Lee, T.M. and Ong, B., 2017. Econometric Analysis of a Cryptocurrency Index for Portfolio Investment. In *Handbook of Blockchain, Digital Finance, and Inclusion, Volume 1* (pp. 175-206).

Chohan, U., (2017). *Initial Coin Offerings (ICOs): Risks, Regulation, and Accountability*.

Chuen, K., David, L.E.E., Guo, L. and Wang, Y., (2017). *Cryptocurrency: A New Investment Opportunity?*.

Corbet, S., Larkin, C., Lucey, B., Meegan, A. and Yarovaya, L., (2017). *Cryptocurrency Reaction to FOMC Announcements: Evidence of Heterogeneity Based on Blockchain Stack Position.*

Deepika, E.P.E. and Kaur, E.R., (2017) *Cryptocurrency: Trends, Perspectives and Challenges.*

DiPiero, C., (2017). *Deciphering Cryptocurrency: Shining a Light on the Deep Dark Web. U. Ill.* L. Rev., p.1267.

Dwyer, G.P., (2015). The economics of Bitcoin and similar private digital currencies. *Journal of Financial Stability, 17,* pp.81-91.

Gamble, C., (2017). *The Legality and Regulatory Challenges of Decentralised Crypto-Currency: A Western Perspective. Int'l Trade & Bus.* L. Rev., 20, p.346.

Garay, J.A., (2017). Basic Properties of the Blockchain: (Invited Talk). *In Proceedings of the ACM Workshop on Blockchain,*

Cryptocurrencies and Contracts (pp. 1-1). ACM.

Graydon, C., (2014). *What is Cryptocurrency?* p.2017.

Hacker, P. and Thomale, C., (2017). *Crypto-Securities Regulation: ICOs, Token Sales and Cryptocurrencies under EU Financial Law.*

Haferkorn, M. and Diaz, J.M.Q., (2014). Seasonality and Interconnectivity Within Cryptocurrencies-An Analysis on the Basis of Bitcoin, Litecoin and Namecoin. In *International Workshop on Enterprise Applications and Services in the Finance Industry* (pp. 106-120). Springer, Cham.

Hayes, A.S., (2016). Cryptocurrency value formation: An empirical study leading to a cost of production model for valuing bitcoin. *Telematics and Informatics.*

Hegadekatti, K. and SG, Y., (2017). *Kibbutz Economy Interactions with Blockchains and Cryptocurrency Networks.*

Heller, D., (2017). 17-13 *Do Digital Currencies Pose a Threat to Sovereign Currencies and Central Banks?.*

Hsieh, Y.Y., Vergne, J.P. and Wang, S., (2017). *The Internal and External Governance of Blockchain-Based Organizations: Evidence from Cryptocurrencies.*

Kowkutla, V. and Ravi, S., (2017). *Security Standards for Embedded Devices and Systems. In Fundamentals of IP and SoC Security (pp. 295-311). Springer International Publishing.*

Krause, D. and Pham, N., (2017). *Bitcoin a favourable instrument for diversification?: A quantitative study on the relations between Bitcoin and global stock markets.*

Litke, P. and Stewart, J., (2014). *BGP hijacking for cryptocurrency profit.*

Mitzenmacher, M., (2017). *Building a better hash function: technical perspective. Communications of the ACM, 60(7), pp.93-93.*

Mokhtarian, E. and Lindgren, A., (2017). *Rise of the Crypto Hedge Fund: Operational Issues and Best Practices for Institutional Cryptocurrency Trading.*

Narayanan, A., Bonneau, J., Felten, E., Miller, A., and Goldfeder, S., (2016). *Bitcoin and Cryptocurrency Technologies: A*

Comprehensive Introduction. Princeton University Press.

O'Leary, K., O'Reilly, P., Feller, J., Gleasure, R., Li, S. and Cristoforo, J., (2017). Exploring the Application of Blockchain Technology to Combat the Effects of Social Loafing in Cross Functional Group Projects. *In Proceedings of the 13th International Symposium on Open Collaboration* (p. 13). ACM.

Peck, M.E., (2017). Blockchains: How they work and why they'll change the world. *IEEE Spectrum, 54*(10), pp.26-35.

Peterson, D., (2017). *Digital Currencies: Unlocking the Secrets of Crypto-Currencies*. Partridge Publishing Singapore.

Qiu, S., Wang, B., Li, M., Liu, J. and Shi, Y., (2017). Toward Practical Privacy-Preserving Frequent Itemset Mining on Encrypted Cloud Data. *IEEE Transactions on Cloud Computing*.

Sharma, S.K., Krishma, N.N. and Raina, E.C., (2017). *Survey Paper on Cryptocurrency*.

Sheehan, D., Gleasure, R., Feller, J., O'Reilly, P., Li, S. and Cristiforo, J., (2017). Does Miner Pooling Impact Bitcoin's Ability to

Stay Decentralized?. *In Proceedings of the 13th International Symposium on Open Collaboration* (p. 25). ACM.

Shmueli, G., Bruce, P.C., Yahav, I., Patel, N.R. and Lichtendahl Jr, K.C., (2017). *Data Mining for Business Analytics: Concepts, Techniques, and Applications in R. John Wiley & Sons.*

Solat, S. and Potop-Butucaru, M., (2017). Brief Announcement: ZeroBlock: *Timestamp-Free Prevention of Block-Withholding Attack in Bitcoin. In International Symposium on Stabilization, Safety, and Security of Distributed Systems* (pp. 356-360). Springer, Cham.

Sun, J., Qin, J. and Ma, J., (2017). *Securely Outsourcing Decentralized Multi-authority Attribute Based Signature. In International Symposium on Cyberspace Safety and Security* (pp. 86-102). Springer, Cham.

Surowiecki, J., (2011).

Cryptocurrency. *Technology review, 114*(5), pp.106-107.

Tennant, L., (2017). Improving the Anonymity of the IOTA Cryptocurrency.

Verma, D., Desai, N., Preece, A. and Taylor, I., (2017). A blockchain based architecture for asset management in coalition operations. *In SPIE Defense+ Security* (pp. 101900Y-101900Y). International Society for Optics and Photonics.

Vigna, P. and Casey, M.J., (2016). *The age of cryptocurrency: how bitcoin and the blockchain are challenging the global economic order*. Macmillan.

Vranken, H., (2017). Sustainability of bitcoin and blockchains. *Current Opinion in Environmental Sustainability, 28*, pp.1-9.

Walker, M., (2017). *Blockchain and bitcoin: In search of a critique*. LSE Business Review.

Williams, D., (2017). *Cryptocurrency Compendium: A Reference for Digital Currencies: A Reference for Digital Currencies*. Lulu.

Xiang, F., Huaimin, W., Peichang, S., Yingwei, F. and Yijie, W., (2017). JCLedger: A Blockchain Based Distributed Ledger for JointCloud Computing. In Distributed Computing Systems Workshops (ICDCSW), 2017 *IEEE 37th International Conference* on (pp. 289-293). IEEE.

Yadav, M., (2017). Exploring Signals for Investing in an Initial Coin Offering (ICO).

Yu, G. and Zhang, J., (2017). *Revisit Capital Controls Policies When Bitcoin Is in Town.*

Zetzsche, D., Buckley, R., Arner, D. and Föhr, L., (2017). *The ICO Gold Rush: It's a Scam, It's a Bubble, It's a Super Challenge for Regulators.*

Zhang, R. and Preneel, B., (2017). On the Necessity of a Prescribed Block Validity Consensus: Analyzing Bitcoin Unlimited Mining Protocol. *In International Conference on emerging Networking EXperiments and Technologies-CoNEXT* 2017. ACM.

Zhao, J., Liu, J., Qin, Z. and Ren, K., (2017). Privacy Protection Scheme Based on Remote Anonymous Attestation for Trusted Smart Meters. *IEEE Transactions on Smart Grid.*

Zima, M., (2017). Coincer: Decentralised Trustless Platform for Exchanging Decentralised Cryptocurrencies. *In International Conference on Network and System Security* (pp. 672-682). Springer, Cham.

Zimmer, Z., (2017). Bitcoin and Potosí Silver: Historical *Perspectives on Cryptocurrency. Technology and culture, 58*(2), pp.307-334.

www.ingramcontent.com/pod-product-compliance
Lightning Source LLC
Chambersburg PA
CBHW071231220526
45468CB00002B/800